THE ULTIMATE
MOVIE
QUOTE
QUIZ BOOK

Jack Goldstein

Published in 2017 by
Acorn Books
www.acornbooks.co.uk

Acorn Books is an imprint of
Andrews UK Limited
www.andrewsuk.com

Copyright © 2017 Jack Goldstein

CONTENTS

INTRODUCTION

How well do you know your movies? Do you think you could recognize a film from just one key line? If so, you'll love this fantastic quiz, featuring famous (and some not-so-famous) quotes from over four hundred different films.

The quiz is split into three main difficulties: easy, medium and hard. Within each difficulty there are both decade-specific rounds and general sections, in which the films referenced could come from any year between 1970 and 2017.

Some quotes contain language that could be considered a *little* above PG level, although we have blanked out the middle letters of the worst words used.

So if you think you're ready for the quiz, prince of a thousand enemies, then dance, magic dance – because nobody puts Baby in a corner. After all, this is Sparta... Toga! Toga! Toga!

Enjoy the quiz!

THE QUIZ

THE QUOTES

Easy – The 1970s

1.   I know what you're thinking. "Did he fire six shots or only five?" Well to tell you the truth in all this excitement I kinda lost track myself.

2.   All the world will be your enemy, prince of a thousand enemies. And when they catch you, they will kill you.

3.   I would like, if I may, to take you on a strange journey.

4.   Would ya just watch the hair. Ya know, I work on my hair a long time and you hit it. He hits my hair.

5.   Listen, everybody! There's no limit to how high we can fly! We can dive for fish and never have to live on garbage again!

6.   Micro changes in air density, my a**.

7.   Hokey religions and ancient weapons are no match for a good blaster at your side, kid.

8.   A deer has to be taken with one shot. I try to tell people that but they don't listen.

9.   All those things I can do. All those powers. And I couldn't even save him.

10.   Listen, Friar, you're mighty preachy and you're gonna preach your neck right into a hangman's noose.

11.   TOGA! TOGA!

12.   I am the Nightrider. I'm a fuel injected suicide machine. I am the rocker, I am the roller, I am the out-of-controller!

13.   Don't you see that killing me is not going to bring back your apples?

14. Look at me, Damien! It's all for you.

15. We aren't dealing with ordinary machines here. These are highly complicated pieces of equipment. Almost as complicated as living organisms. In some cases, they have been designed by other computers. We don't know exactly how they work.

16. I love the smell of napalm in the morning!

17. Let me come with you, Pontiuth. I may be of thome athithtanthe if there ith a thudden crithith!

18. Every dead body that is not exterminated becomes one of them. It gets up and kills! The people it kills get up and kill!

19. You know... I'll bet those golden tickets make the chocolate taste terrible.

20. I am honoured and grateful that you have invited me to your home on the wedding day of your daughter. And may their first child be a masculine child.

Turn to page 46 for the answers

Easy – General Part 1

21. We are cursed men, Miss Turner.

22. I use antlers in all of my decorating.

23. Blurr, get the Dinobots in the shuttle.

24. Must go faster! Must go faster!

25. If only you could see what I've seen with your eyes.

26. This one goes to eleven.

27. It's not a tumor.

28. Somebody stop me!

29. You probably heard we ain't in the prisoner-takin' business; we in the killin' Nazi business. And cousin, business is a-boomin'.

30. Kneel before Zod.

31. Houston, we have a problem.

32. I'll be back!

33. That'll do, pig, that'll do.

34. A 'Royale' with cheese!

35. Uh, I'm not very hungry; just gimme a double Polar burger wit' everything and a cherry soda wit' chocolate ice cream.

36. Oh, shucks, Napoleon. That ain't nothin' more but a little ol' cricket bug.

37.   Number Five is alive.

38.   I love lamp.

39.   No, I am your father.

40.   He says the sun came out last night. He says it sang to him.

Turn to page 47 for the answers

Easy – The 1980s

41. Your ego's writing checks your body can't cash.

42. Get away from her, you bitch.

43. Wax on, wax off.

44. What is your major malfunction, numbnuts?

45. Here's Johnny!

46. Dance, magic dance.

47. They're here...

48. It's 106 miles to Chicago, we got a full tank of gas, half a pack of cigarettes, it's dark, and we're wearing sunglasses.

49. Nobody puts Baby in a corner.

50. Your mother was a hamster and your father smelled of elderberries!

51. Oh God! The dog wet on the picnic basket.

52. There can be only one!

53. Remember how I said I'd kill you last? I lied.

54. Kali Ma... Kali Ma.

55. Where we're going, we don't need roads.

56. I aint got time to bleed!

57. I have the *Power*!

58.   I am not an animal! I am a human being!

59.   You guys wanna go see a dead body?

60.   I love the smell of napalm in the morning.

Turn to page 48 for the answers

61.   Yippee-ki-yay...

62.   Heeeey yoooou guuuuuys!

63.   Never send a human to do a machine's job.

64.   If you build it, they will come.

65.   The power of Christ compels you!

66.   I am the shadow on the moon at night, filling your dreams to the brim with fright.

67.   Tell you what... truth is, sometimes I miss you so bad I can hardly stand it...

68.   If there is a war on drugs, then many of our family members are the enemy. And I don't know how you wage war on your own family.

69.   Riddle me this and riddle me that, who's afraid of the big bad bat?

70.   they may take our lives, but they will never take our freedom.

71.   Let's play global thermonuclear war.

72.   Hi, I'm Chucky. Wanna play?

73.   I bet you can squeal like a pig. Weeeeeeee!

74.   Elliot!

75. Fear is the path to the dark side. Fear leads to anger. Anger leads to hate. Hate leads to suffering. I sense much fear in you.

76. I'm the king of the world!

77. You complete me.

78. I am serious, and don't call me Shirley.

79. Ever since I was a young boy, I've played the silver ball. From Soho down to Brighton, I must have played them all.

80. But if you don't, I will look for you, I will find you, and I will kill you.

Turn to page 49 for the answers

81. Is that hair gel?

82. As far back as I can remember, I always wanted to be a gangster.

83. Never let anyone know what you are thinking.

84. Danger, Will Robinson, danger.

85. Here are your names: Mr. Brown, Mr. White, Mr. Blonde, Mr. Blue, Mr. Orange, and Mr. Pink.

86. My CPU is a neuro-net processor, a learning computer.

87. I have been stabbed, shot, poisoned, frozen, hung, electrocuted, and burned.

88. To infinity, and beyond!

89. I ate his liver with some fava beans and a nice Chianti.

90. Oh, as I hold this cold meat, I'm reminded of Winston.

91. Good morning... Oh, and in case I don't see ya, good afternoon, good evening, and good night!

92. Whoever saves one life, saves the world entire.

93. I see dead people.

94. The greatest trick the devil ever pulled was convincing the world he didn't exist.

95. Run, Forrest, run.

96. Do I make you horny, baby?

97. Once the bus goes fifty miles an hour, the bomb is armed.

98. I'm afraid to close my eyes, I'm afraid to open them.

99. You can't handle the truth!

100. In the name of the father, the son and the holy goat.

Turn to page 50 for the answers

101. Wilson!

102. When it's over, your phone rings, someone knows you watched the tape... and what they say is, 'You will die in seven days'.

103. I must break you.

104. Ack! Ack! Ack!

105. Say hello to my little friend!

106. What's your favorite scary movie?

107. That furball is my son, and your future king!

108. I know you are but what am I?

109. The draft is white people sending black people to make war on the yellow people to defend the land they stole from the red people!

110. You know, I'm a rather brilliant surgeon. Perhaps I can help you with that hump.

111. That's the Chicago way, and that's how you get Capone.

112. Loneliness has followed me my whole life, everywhere. In bars, in cars, sidewalks, stores, everywhere. There's no escape. I'm God's lonely man.

113. That'll do, Donkey. That'll do.

114. My father taught me many things here – he taught me in this room. He taught me: keep your friends close, but your enemies closer.

115. Life moves pretty fast. You don't stop and look around once in a while, you could miss it.

116. This thing is much too big to be some lost dinosaur.

117. I love you, Will, beyond poetry.

118. And this one time, at band camp...

119. Drop that stereo before I blow your goddamn nuts off, a**hole.

120. It's a funny world we live in. Speaking of which, do you know how I got these scars?

Turn to page 51 for the answers

121. This is the Ocean, silly, we're not the only two in here.

122. Sand is overrated. It's just tiny, little rocks.

123. Remember, with great power comes great responsibility.

124. I can guarantee the closest shave you'll ever know.

125. Who the hell is this organisation Bond? How can they be everywhere and we know nothing about them!

126. Come in with the milk. Come in with the milk. Come in with the milk.

127. Legend tells of a legendary warrior whose kung fu skills were the stuff of legend.

128. I am McLovin.

129. Trinity. I know you can hear me. I'm never letting go. I can't. I just love you too damn much.

130. At my signal, unleash hell.

131. You're a wizard, Harry!

132. Silly caucasian girl likes to play with Samurai swords.

133. I don't think there will be a return journey, Mr. Frodo.

134. Voilà! In view, a humble vaudevillian veteran, cast vicariously as both victim and villain by the vicissitudes of fate. This visage, no mere veneer of vanity, is a vestige of the vox populi, now vacant, vanished.

135. Dammit, man! I'm a doctor, not a physicist!

136. What's the last thing that you do remember?

137. Spider-Pig, Spider-Pig. Does whatever a Spider-Pig does.

138. You found Wonka's last golden ticket! In my shop, too!

139. That is one big damn tree!

140. This... is... *Sparta*!

Turn to page 52 for the answers

141. If you feel you are not properly sedated, call 348-844 immediately. Failure to do so may result in prosecution for criminal drug evasion.

142. Each of us... at some time in our lives, turns to someone – a father, a brother, a God... and asks... "Why am I here? What was I meant to be?"

143. My late husband played the violin. Not professionally, but he was very good. He once played the Minute Waltz in 58 seconds.

144. Are those guys coming after me? Those guys are coming after me.

145. We came here from a dying world. We drift through the universe, from planet to planet, pushed on by the solar winds. We adapt and we survive. The function of life is survival.

146. All right, Popeye's here! Get your hands on your heads, get off the bar, and get on the wall!

147. In my situation, days are like women – each one's so damn precious, but they all end up leaving you.

148. That's some bad hat, Harry.

149. Andrew... remember... be sure and tell them... it was only a bloody game.

150. You have offended my family and you have offended the Shaolin Temple.

151. I met him, fifteen years ago. I was told there was nothing left; no reason, no conscience, no understanding; and even the most rudimentary sense of life or death, of good or evil, right or wrong.

152. I was cured, all right!

153. Total submission. That's what I like in a woman – total submission.

154. All right, all right, and yes-sirree! A clean hit! A perfect hit! And no pain for the target. Too bad the guy was only thirty-eight; just two years older, he'd have been worth three times the points.

155. I think he's attempting re-entry, sir.

156. He betrayed me, he betrayed you, he betrayed the Aryan race!

157. I'm as mad as hell, and I'm not going to take this any more!

158. Treguna, Makoidees, Trecorum, Sadis Dee!

159. He's just another scripture thumping hack from Galilee.

160. A relationship, I think, is like a shark. You know? It has to constantly move forward or it dies. And I think what we got on our hands is a dead shark.

Turn to page 53 for the answers

161. I'm just a girl, standing in front of a boy, asking him to love her.

162. Ray, if someone asks you if you are a god, you say yes!

163. I'm not bad. I'm just drawn that way.

164. If he gets up, we'll all get up, it'll be anarchy!

165. See that clock on the wall? In five minutes you are not going to believe what I've told you.

166. Why don't you knock it off with them negative waves? Why don't you dig how beautiful it is out here? Why don't you say something righteous and hopeful for a change?

167. I never f****d anybody over in my life didn't have it coming to them.

168. May the forks be with us.

169. It's talking, Merry. The tree is talking.

170. In one of the countless billions of galaxies in the universe, lies a medium-sized star, and one of its satellites, a green and insignificant planet, is now dead.

171. I am your father's brother's nephew's cousin's former roommate.

172. Get off my plane.

173. I want the fairy tale.

174. If it bleeds, we can kill it.

175. Father, are you sure she's a supreme being?

176. It's over, Johnny.

177. Now you're looking for the secret. But you won't find it because of course, you're not really looking. You don't really want to work it out. You want to be fooled.

178. Attention all units in the San Pedro, Long Beach, Torrance and Carson areas. Stand-by to copy. Long Beach PD is in pursuit of a 1973 Ford Mustang, yellow in color.

179. Lord, place the steel of the Holy Spirit in my spine and the love of the Virgin Mary in my heart.

180. It puts the lotion in the basket!

Turn to page 54 for the answers

181. I'll have what she's having.

182. China is here? China is here? I don't even know what the hell that means!

183. I'm not gonna to stand here and listen to this baloney!

184. Carpe Diem. Seize the day, boys.

185. We'd better get back, 'cause it'll be dark soon, and they mostly come at night... mostly.

186. That was Gary Cooper, a**hole!

187. I think the carrot infinitely more fascinating than the geranium.

188. Suck my fat one, you cheap dime-store hood.

189. I may be wet, but my martini is still dry.

190. Now that you're dead, what are you going to do with the rest of your life?

191. I'm washing lettuce. Soon, I'll be on fries. In a few years, I'll make assistant manager, and that's when the big bucks start rolling in.

192. Do as I say and I'll be your slave forever.

193. There's only two things you've got going for yourself in this town. Jack and s**t. And Jack just left town.

194. I coulda been a contender.

195. You keep a horse in the basement?

196. If you give up your dreams, you die.

197. If you give extra kisses, you get bigger hugs!

198. One must usually go to a bowling alley to meet women of such stature.

199. Do you have anything besides Mexican food?

200. My blood is in your veins.

Turn to page 55 for the answers

201. We're looking for the man with the hands.

202. You don't frighten us with your silly knees-bent running around advancing behavior!

203. I have lived three hundred years, and I long to die. But death is no longer possible. I am immortal. I present now my story, full of mystery and intrigue – rich in irony, and most satirical. It is set deep in a possible future, so none of these events have yet occurred, but they *may.*

204. Yeah, I can fly.

205. You really are a guppy.

206. I am Cornholio. I need TP for my Bunghole!

207. Mmmmmm, Juicy Fruit.

208. How'd you do it, Frank? How did you cheat on the bar exam in Louisiana?

209. 97X, Bam! the future of rock and roll!

210. Gentlemen, the lunchbox has landed!

211. Remember what the general said; we're the cavalry. It would be bad form to arrive in advance of schedule. In the nick of time would do nicely.

212. It's just been revoked!

213. Be afraid. Be very afraid.

214. You got the wrong guy. I'm the Dude, man.

215.   Now put it back in. It's only a piece of meat.

216.   If I wanted a joke I'd follow you into the john.

217.   My mind is a raging torrent, flooded with rivulets of thought cascading into a waterfall of creative alternatives.

218.   You wanna get nuts? Let's get nuts!

219.   It's like finding a needle in a stack of needles.

220.   I can be your best friend or your worst enemy. You seem to prefer the latter.

Turn to page 56 for the answers

221. I think this boy's cheese has done slid off his cracker.

222. George has fashioned me a metal fingertip, I am quite the town freak which satisfies!

223. You know, you drive almost slow enough to drive Miss Daisy.

224. Tic-tac, sir?

225. You know what the difference is between you and me? I make this look good!

226. Let's kick some ice!

227. She's magically babelicious.

228. I guess that was your accomplice in the wood chipper?

229. I'm not even supposed to be here today.

230. In the future, when a woman is crying like that, she isn't having any fun.

231. I got to get me one of these!

232. Wowser!

233. I'm fifty-six years old. I can't blame anybody else for something I did.

234. When your little girl is on the slab, where will it tickle you?

235. Look at me, jerking off in the shower. This will be the high point of my day. It's all downhill from here.

236. He's experienced about as much pain and suffering as anyone I've encountered, give or take, and he still has Hell to look forward to.

237. I eat because I'm unhappy, and I'm unhappy because I eat.

238. I am a star. I'm a star, I'm a star, I'm a star. I am a big, bright, shining star. That's right.

239. And you must be the monopoly guy!

240. I crap bigger than you!

Turn to page 57 for the answers

241. It's only after we've lost everything that we're free to do anything.

242. The dress is for sale. I'm not.

243. We'll see who's powerless now!

244. This warehouse is where you and your government have hidden all of your secrets, yes?

245. Can you believe it? We're in the middle of a drought, and the water commissioner drowns. Only in L.A.

246. Hey bartender, know how to make a red eye?

247. I don't know. Maybe they just oughta leave it the way it is. Kind of a shrine to all the bulls**t in the world.

248. At the end of this day, one shall stand, one shall fall!

249. Never give up and good luck will find you.

250. I believe you have my stapler.

251. I'm your number one fan. There's nothing to worry about.

252. Not to be rude or anything, but this isn't a great time for me to have a house elf in my bedroom.

253. This don't look like no expressway to me.

254. I should have stayed at home and played with myself!

255. The moment we stop fighting for each other, that's the moment we lose our humanity.

256. I know a cool place in the desert.

257. Stop calling me Warren, my name isn't f**king Warren!

258. Hello. My name is Inigo Montoya. You killed my father. Prepare to die.

259. Would you like to talk about a possible lunch trade?

260. Hope is a dangerous thing. Hope can drive a man insane.

Turn to page 58 for the answers

261. When I was your age they would say we can become cops, or criminals. Today, what I'm saying to you is this: when you're facing a loaded gun, what's the difference?

262. A sword by itself rules nothing. It only comes alive in skilled hands.

263. In other news... The dead walk the earth!

264. The hunt is his obsession. He's never gonna stop!

265. There has to be a mathematical explanation for how bad that tie is.

266. When somebody asks me a question, I tell them the answer.

267. 28 days, 6 hours, 42 minutes, 12 seconds. That is when the world will end.

268. You're an inanimate f***ing object!

269. Now I don't hear as good as I used to and I forget stuff and I aint as pretty as I used to be but god damn it I'm still standing here and I'm The Ram.

270. Now raise your goblet of rock. It's a toast to those who rock!

271. Aw, hells bells. They even shot the dog!

272. Not even the younglings survived.

273. No matter how many times you save the world, it always manages to get back in jeopardy again.

274. You sit on a throne of lies!

275. I want to play a game.

276. Sunnyside is a place of ruin and despair, ruled by an evil bear who smells of strawberries!

277. Judas... you betray the Son of Man with a kiss?

278. This is an occasion for genuinely tiny knickers.

279. Your mom goes to college.

280. Give 'em a show that's so splendiferous, row after row will grow vociferous.

Turn to page 59 for the answers

281. Willkommen, bienvenue, welcome.

282. Now then, what do we know? One, that Professor Fassbinder and his daughter have been kidnapped. Two, that someone has kidnapped them. Three, that my hand is on fire.

283. I'm sure the over-burdened British taxpayer would be fascinated to know how its Special Ordinances section disperses its funds. In future, Commander, let me suggest a perfectly adequate watchmaker just down the street.

284. Most of them died instantly, but a few had time to go quietly nuts.

285. For the good old American life: For the money, for the glory, and for the fun... mostly for the money.

286. Ooooo – chicken delight! Well that's what I call some pretty good smotherin' cousin.

287. Ten thousand light years from nowhere, our planets shot to pieces, people starving, and I'm gonna get us in trouble? What the matter with you? I tell you... yeah, well, we may as well live for today! We might not have many left!

288. You guys are about to write a story that says the former Attorney General, the highest-ranking law enforcement officer in this country, is a crook! Just be sure you're right.

289. You could have dinner with us... my brother makes good head cheese! You like head cheese?

290. I don't wanna be the same as everybody else. That's why I'm a Mod, see? I mean, you gotta be somebody, ain't ya, or you might as well jump in the sea and drown.

291. Listen, Snow White. Me and you gonna tangle, sooner or later. Did you hear what I say?

292. I'll just die if I don't get this recipe. I'll just die if I don't get this recipe. I'll just die if I don't get this recipe.

293. I know, I know. We are Your chosen people. But, once in a while, can't You choose someone else?

294. Your boss is quite a card player, Mr. Kelly; how does he do it?

295. You ever seen a duck that couldn't swim? Quack, quack!

296. The Andrea Doria stayed afloat ten hours before she sank.

297. You're gonna eat lightnin' and you're gonna crap thunder!

298. They don't look like Presbyterians to me.

299. If you disobey the rules of society, they send you to prison; if you disobey the rules of the prison, they send you to us.

300. Oh, come on. If I've got to watch my language just because they let a few broads in, I'm going to quit. How the hell can you run a goddamn railroad without swearing?

Turn to page 60 for the answers

HARD – GENERAL PART 1

301. He's a pepper, she's a pepper, wouldn't you like to be a pepper.

302. In this situation mediocrity and genius are equally useless! I must tell you that we really have no desire to conquer any cosmos. We want to extend the Earth up to its borders. We don't know what to do with other worlds. We don't need other worlds. We need a mirror.

303. I'm pretty sure there's a lot more to life than being really, really, ridiculously good looking.

304. Everything's green on my screen, skipper.

305. I'm the guy who keeps Mr. Dead in his pocket.

306. Sometimes the world of the living gets mixed up with the world of the dead.

307. You never open your mouth until you know what the shot is.

308. Fear causes hesitation, and hesitation will cause your worst fears to come true.

309. I have a sadness shield that keeps out all the sadness, and it's big enough for all of us.

310. Vanity is definitely my favorite sin.

311. The best way you hurt rich people is by turning them into poor people.

312. So at last we meet for the first time for the last time.

313. You scratched my cd, you picked it up in clear daylight and scratched it.

314. Now if you'll excuse me, I'm going to go on an overnight drunk, and in 10 days I'm going to set out to find the shark that ate my friend and destroy it. Anyone who wants to tag along is more than welcome.

315. Mom, that salesman is on TV!

316. Soon as I get home, the first thing I'm gonna do is punch your momma in the mouth!

317. Rick, it's the Nineties. Can't afford to be afraid of our own people anymore, man.

318. Give me some sugar Baby!

319. Well I'm not a scientist. But I know all things begin and end in eternity.

320. A surprising number of human beings are without purpose, though it is probable that they are performing some function unknown to themselves.

Turn to page 61 for the answers

321. We have weak trees.

322. I've seen the Exorcist 67 times and it keeps getting funnier every single time I see it.

323. You're not dying, you just cant think of anything good to do!

324. He's trying to kill me! I asked for the salted nuts. He brought me the unsalted nuts. The unsalted nuts make me choke!

325. Listen... you smell something?

326. He had to split.

327. Looks like a gelfling, smells like a gelfling, maybe you are a gelfling.

328. I can't believe I gave my panties to a geek!

329. You know, you're kinda not so bad looking when your face isn't messin it up.

330. Who's laughing now, huh? Who's laughing now?

331. If you had any idea of the true nature of the universe, any at all, you would have hidden from it in terror.

332. Excuse me, I have to go. Somewhere there is a crime happening.

333. Why don't we just wait here for a little while... see what happens...

334. I'm going to teach you to hate spending money.

335. The rich. You know why they're so odd? Because they can afford to be.

336. You're right, Johnny, you can't win no matter what you do.

337. This is what my girlfriend would look like without skin.

338. Life all comes down to a few moments. This is one of them.

339. Strange things are afoot at the Circle K.

340. Ponce!

Turn to page 62 for the answers

341. I can't marry Ryan. Eww.

342. I've got to get to a library... Fast!

343. Linda, go get my guitar. It's out there with that looney toon.

344. Some cultures are defined by their relationship with cheese.

345. Spatula City!

346. A little nonsense now and then is relished by the wisest men.

347. I wanna let them know they didnt break me.

348. Hi, I'm Fred. I like tacos and '71 Cabernet.

349. I watched C-beams glitter in the dark near the Tannhauser gate.

350. It's not the years, it's the mileage.

351. Does Elvis talk to you?

352. We are creatures of the spring, you and I.

353. A dead person breathed on me!

354. Unlike the Greek, England has no true mythology. All we have are witches and fairies.

355. This is where the law stops, and I start.

356. Welcome humans! I am ready for you.

357. I shall serve no fries before their time.

358. Christine is dead. She is dead! Dead! Dead! Dead! Dead! Dead!

359. Sometimes you just gotta say, "What the f**k!"

360. To the winch, wench.

Turn to page 63 for the answers

361. I've fallen for you like a blind roofer.

362. Promise me you'll come back for me.

363. There is no normal.

364. I'm only an elected official here, I can't make decisions by myself!

365. I've been very lonely in my isolated tower of indecipherable speech.

366. Real loss is only possible when you love something more than you love yourself.

367. Are you people insane? I'm the director. I make the casting decisions around here.

368. I can't look. Could somebody please cover my eyes?

369. If you were yogurt, would you be fruit at the bottom, or stirred?

370. Any man don't wanna get killed better clear on out the back.

371. It's quiet. Only three days left. Plenty of time to read my Bible and look for a loophole.

372. You people. If there isn't a movie about it, it's not worth knowing, is it?

373. Look upon me! I'll show you the life of the mind!

374. He knows a lot about Sean Connery.

375. You're a virgin who can't drive.

376. The only thing I like integrated is my coffee.

377. I don't do drugs though, just weed.

378. You can take away our phones and you can take away our keys, but you can *not* take away our dreams.

379. We've got cows.

380. It's dangerous to confuse children with angels.

Turn to page 64 for the answers

381. Get off my lawn.

382. The underprivileged are beating our goddamned brains out. You know what I say? Stick them in concentration camps, that's what I say.

383. Passion, you see, can be destroyed by a doctor. It cannot be created.

384. And the moral of the story is... if you walking on eggs, don't hop!

385. In this world, a man, himself, is nothing. And there ain't no world but this one.

386. You are evil, and you must be destroyed.

387. It ain't the size that counts, a**hole, it's what ya do with it!

388. First we crack the shell. Then, we crack the nuts inside.

389. Did I listen to pop music because I was miserable? Or was I miserable because I listened to pop music?

390. Which would be worse, to live as a monster, or to die as a good man?

391. I want the future to be unknown. I want to become a whole person.

392. You ooze, you lose.

393. Sir, you are a vulgarian.

394. I got good news and bad news, girls. The good news is your dates are here.

395. My place is with you. I go where you go.

396. If you look around the table and you can't tell who the sucker is, it's you.

397. This river can kill you in a thousand ways.

398. We seem to be made to suffer. It's our lot in life.

399. This is the '90s. You can't just walk up and slap a guy, you have to say something cool first.

400. You need more than guts to be a good gangster. You need ideas.

Turn to page 65 for the answers

401. I know who I am. I'm the dude thats playin' the dude disguised as another dude.

402. I drink your milkshake!

403. I'm just a simple man, trying to make my way in the universe.

404. This box is full of stuff that almost killed me.

405. This is not a war any more than there's a war between men and maggots...this is an extermination.

406. A child's voice, however honest and true, is meaningless to those who've forgotten how to listen.

407. The greatest thing you'll ever learn is just to love and be loved in return.

408. Nobody makes me bleed my own blood...nobody!

409. I'm saying that when the President does it, it's not illegal!

410. I will look on your treasures, gypsy. Is this understood?

411. What business is it of yours where I come from, friendo?

412. We bury our sins here, Dave. We wash them clean.

413. Tell Graham... see. Tell him to see. And tell Merrill to swing away.

414. For the first time in my life, I got people respecting me. Please, don't ask me to give it up.

415. I made a promise, Mr Frodo. A promise.

416. I love to see a woman playing the cello.

417. I'm just one stomach flu away from my goal weight.

418. Tigers love pepper. They hate cinnamon.

419. Now I've asked you forty different ways and it's time you come up with a fresh answer.

420. Nobody asks to be a hero, it just sometimes turns out that way.

Turn to page 66 for the answers

THE ANSWERS

EASY – THE 1970S

1. Dirty Harry

2. Watership Down

3. The Rocky Horror Picture Show

4. Saturday Night Fever

5. Jonathan Livingston Seagull

6. Alien

7. Star Wars: Episode IV – A New Hope

8. The Deer Hunter

9. Superman

10. Robin Hood

11. Animal House

12. Mad Max

13. The Wicker Man

14. The Omen

15. Westworld

16. Apocalypse Now

17. Life of Brian

18. Dawn of the Dead

19. Willy Wonka & the Chocolate Factory

20. The Godfather

EASY – GENERAL PART 1

21. Pirates of the Caribbean: The Curse of the Black Pearl

22. Beauty and the Beast

23. Transformers: The Movie

24. Jurassic Park

25. Blade Runner

26. Spinal Tap

27. Kindergarten Cop

28. The Mask

29. Inglourious Basterds

30. Superman II

31. Apollo 13

32. The Terminator

33. Babe

34. Pulp Fiction

35. Grease

36. The Aristocats

37. Short Circuit

38. Anchorman

39. The Empire Strikes Back

40. Close Encounters of the Third Kind

EASY – THE 1980S

41. Top Gun

42. Aliens

43. The Karate Kid

44. Full Metal Jacket

45. The Shining

46. Labyrinth

47. Poltergeist

48. The Blues Brothers

49. Dirty Dancing

50. Monty Python and the Holy Grail

51. National Lampoon's Vacation

52. Highlander

53. Commando

54. Indiana Jones and the Temple of Doom

55. Back to the Future

56. Predator

57. Masters of the Universe

58. The Elephant Man

59. Stand By Me

60. Apocalypse Now

EASY – GENERAL PART 2

61. Die Hard

62. The Goonies

63. The Matrix

64. Field of Dreams

65. The Exorcist

66. The Nightmare Before Christmas

67. Brokeback Mountain

68. Traffic

69. Batman Returns

70. Braveheart

71. WarGames

72. Child's Play

73. Deliverance

74. E.T.

75. Star Wars Episode One: The Phantom Menace

76. Titanic

77. Jerry Maguire

78. Airplane

79. Tommy

80. Taken

EASY – THE 1990S

81. There's Something About Mary

82. Goodfellas

83. The Godfather Part III

84. Lost in Space

85. Reservoir Dogs

86. Terminator 2: Judgement Day

87. Groundhog Day

88. Toy Story

89. The Silence of the Lambs

90. Mrs. Doubtfire

91. The Truman Show

92. Schindler's List

93. The Sixth Sense

94. The Usual Suspects

95. Forrest Gump

96. Austin Powers

97. Speed

98. The Blair Witch Project

99. A Few Good Men

100. Four Weddings and a Funeral

EASY – GENERAL PART 3

101. Cast Away

102. The Ring

103. Rocky IV

104. Mars Attacks

105. Scarface

106. Scream

107. The Lion King

108. Pee-wee's Big Adventure

109. Hair

110. Young Frankenstein

111. The Untouchables

112. Taxi Driver

113. Shrek

114. The Godfather: Part II

115. Ferris Bueller's Day Off

116. Godzilla

117. Shakespeare in Love

118. American Pie

119. Police Academy

120. The Dark Knight

EASY – THE 2000S

121. Finding Nemo

122. Eternal Sunshine of the Spotless Mind

123. Spiderman

124. Sweeney Todd: The Demon Barber of Fleet Street

125. Quantum of Solace

126. The Aviator

127. Kung Fu Panda

128. Superbad

129. The Matrix Reloaded

130. Gladiator

131. Harry Potter and the Sorceror's / Philosopher's Stone

132. Kill Bill: Vol. 1

133. Lord of the Rings: Return of the King

134. V for Vendetta

135. Star Trek

136. Memento

137. The Simpsons Movie

138. Charlie and the Chocolate Factory

139. Avatar

140. 300

MEDIUM – THE 1970s

141. THX 1138

142. Star Trek: The Motion Picture

143. Airport

144. Every Which Way but Loose

145. Invasion of the Body Snatchers

146. The French Connection

147. Assault on Precinct 13

148. Jaws

149. Sleuth

150. Enter the Dragon

151. Halloween

152. A Clockwork Orange

153. I Spit on your Grave

154. Death Race 2000

155. Moonraker

156. The Boys from Brazil

157. Network

158. Bedknobs and Broomsticks

159. Jesus Christ Superstar

160. Annie Hall

Medium – General Part 1

161. Notting Hill

162. Ghostbusters

163. Who Framed Roger Rabbit

164. The Breakfast Club

165. Blue Velvet

166. Kelly's Heroes

167. Scarface

168. Mystery Men

169. The Lord of the Rings: The Two Towers

170. Beneath the Planet of the Apes

171. Spaceballs

172. Air Force One

173. Pretty Woman

174. Predator

175. The Fifth Element

176. Rambo: First Blood

177. The Prestige

178. Gone in 60 Seconds

179. Gangs of New York

180. The Silence of the Lambs

Medium – The 1980s

181. When Harry Met Sally

182. Big Trouble in Little China

183. Weird Science

184. Dead Poet's Society

185. Aliens

186. Die Hard

187. Withnail and I

188. Stand by Me

189. Never Say Never Again

190. Heathers

191. Coming to America

192. Labyrinth

193. Army of Darkness

194. Raging Bull

195. The Burbs

196. Flashdance

197. Santa Claus: The Movie

198. Arthur

199. The Three Amigos

200. The Lost Boys

201. Edwards Scissorhands

202. Monty Python and the Holy Grail

203. Zardoz

204. Iron Man

205. The Little Mermaid

206. Beavis and Butthead Do America

207. One Flew Over the Cuckoo's Nest

208. Catch Me If You Can

209. Rain Man

210. The Full Monty

211. A Bridge Too Far

212. Lethal Weapon II

213. The Fly

214. The Big Lebowski

215. The Crying Game

216. Planes, Trains and Automobiles

217. Blazing Saddles

218. Batman

219. Saving Private Ryan

220. The Cable Guy

Medium – The 1990s

221. The Green Mile

222. The Piano

223. Bad Boys

224. Dumb and Dumber

225. Men in Black

226. Batman and Robin

227. Wayne's World

228. Fargo

229. Clerks

230. Thelma and Louise

231. Independence Day

232. Inspector Gadget

233. Jackie Brown

234. The Silence of the Lambs

235. American Beauty

236. Se7en

237. Austin Powers: The Spy who Shagged Me

238. Boogie Nights

239. Ace Ventura 2: When Nature Calls

240. City Slickers

241. Fight Club

242. Indecent Proposal

243. WALL-E

244. Indiana Jones and the Kingdom of the Crystal Skull

245. Chinatown

246. Cocktail

247. The Towering Inferno

248. Transformers

249. The Neverending Story

250. Office Space

251. Misery

252. Harry Potter and the Chamber of Secrets

253. The Blues Brothers

254. Caddyshack

255. 2012

256. Leaving Las Vegas

257. Empire Records

258. The Princess Bride

259. Uncle Buck

260. The Shawshank Redemption

MEDIUM – THE 2000s

261. The Departed

262. Crouching Tiger, Hidden Dragon

263. The Corpse Bride

264. Twilight

265. A Beautiful Mind

266. Slumdog Millionaire

267. Donnie Darko

268. In Bruges

269. The Wrestler

270. School of Rock

271. No Country For Old Men

272. Star Wars: Episode III – Revenge of the Sith

273. The Incredibles

274. Elf

275. Saw

276. Toy Story 3

277. The Passion of the Christ

278. Bridget Jones's Diary

279. Napoleon Dynamite

280. Chicago

HARD – THE 1970S

281. Cabaret

282. The Pink Panther Strikes Again

283. Live and Let Die

284. The Andromeda Strain

285. Smokey and the Bandit

286. Play Misty for Me

287. Battlestar Galactica

288. All the President's Men

289. The Texas Chainsaw Massacre

290. Quadrophenia

291. Shaft

292. The Stepford Wives

293. Fiddler on the Roof

294. The Sting

295. Convoy

296. The Poseidon Adventure

297. Rocky

298. The Muppet Movie

299. Escape from Alcatraz

300. The Taking of Pelham One Two Three

Hard – General Part 1

Hard – The 1980s

321. The Money Pit

322. Beetlejuice

323. Ferris Bueller's Day Off

324. Throw Momma from the Train

325. Ghostbusters

326. The Running Man

327. The Dark Crystal

328. Sixteen Candles

329. The Goonies

330. The Evil Dead

331. Flash Gordon

332. Robocop

333. The Thing

334. Brewster's Millions

335. Batman

336. Dirty Dancing

337. Some Kind of Wonderful

338. Wall Street

339. Bill and Ted's Excellent Adventure

340. Withnail and I

HARD – GENERAL PART 2

341. Freaky Friday

342. The Da Vinci Code

343. Sling Blade

344. Benny and Joon

345. UHF

346. Willy Wonka & the Chocolate Factory

347. Pretty in Pink

348. Valley Girl

349. Blade Runner

350. Raiders of the Lost Ark

351. Buffy, The Vampire Slayer

352. Death Becomes Her

353. National Lampoon's Vacation

354. Howards End

355. Cobra

356. Logan's Run

357. Fast Times at Ridgemont High

358. Don't Look Now

359. Risky Business

360. The Neverending Story

Hard – The 1990s

361. Hotshots

362. The English Patient

363. Angus

364. The Nightmare Before Christmas

365. Being John Malkovich

366. Good Will Hunting

367. Ed Wood

368. Toy Story 2

369. Biodome

370. Unforgiven

371. Dead Man Walking

372. Dogma

373. Barton Fink

374. Trainspotting

375. Clueless

376. Malcolm X

377. Half Baked

378. A Night at the Roxbury

379. Twister

380. Magnolia

HARD – GENERAL PART 3

381. Gran Torino

382. Death Wish

383. Equus

384. Blue Thunder

385. The Thin Red Line

386. Steel Magnolias

387. Bride of Chucky

388. Transformers the Movie

389. High Fidelity

390. Shutter Island

391. Twelve Monkeys

392. Mighty Morphin Power Rangers: The Movie

393. A Fish Called Wanda

394. Night of the Creeps

395. Dances With Wolves

396. Quiz Show

397. Anaconda

398. Star Wars: Episode IV – A New Hope

399. The Last Boy Scout

400. City of God

Hard – The 2000s

401. Tropic Thunder

402. There Will Be Blood

403. Star Wars: Episode II – Attack of the Clones

404. The Hurt Locker

405. War of the Worlds

406. Harry Potter and the Prisoner of Azkaban

407. Moulin Rouge

408. Dodgeball

409. Frost/Nixon

410. Borat: Cultural Learnings of America for Make Benefit Glorious Nation of Kazakhstan

411. No Country for Old Men

412. Mystic River

413. Signs

414. Erin Brockovich

415. The Lord of the Rings: The Fellowship of the Ring

416. The Pianist

417. The Devil Wears Prada

418. The Hangover

419. Walk The Line

420. Black Hawk Down

You may also enjoy...

THE ULTIMATE

PUB QUIZ BOOK

1200

QUESTIONS & ANSWERS

JACK GOLDSTEIN

You may also enjoy...

Harry Potter

THE
ULTIMATE
QUIZ BOOK

UNOFFICIAL & UNAUTHORISED

Jack Goldstein

Printed in October 2023
by Rotomail Italia S.p.A., Vignate (MI) - Italy